New Zealand's COASTS

New Zealand's
COASTS

Colin Monteath

Dedicated to the preservation of New Zealand's coastal environments and marine reserves.

David Ling Publishing Limited
PO Box 34601, Birkenhead, Auckland 0746, New Zealand
www.davidling.co.nz
In association with Hedgehog House
www.hedgehoghouse.com

ISBN 978-1-877378-34-8
First Published 2009

Typeset by Express Communications Limited
Printed in China

Front cover: The Archway Islands and Wharariki Beach at sunset. Wharariki is a well-known Golden Bay beach where it is popular to enjoy the peace and solitude of an early morning or evening walk.
Back cover: The kekeno or New Zealand fur seal is surrounded by sea foam as it sits on rocks at the Kaikoura seal colony. Fur seals are commonly found around New Zealand's coastline and they were once hunted for their thick pelt but now enjoy total protection.
Endpapers: Fan shells, Chlamys gemmulata.
Page 1: Sunrise on North Otago's famous Moeraki boulders.
Page 2: This aerial view of Moturua Island in Northland's stunning Bay of Islands gives an appreciation of the beauty of the beaches and waterways around New Zealand's coastline.

◀ *A kekeno or New Zealand fur seal, Artocephalus forsterii, snoozes on warm limestone rocks at Kaikoura.*

"New Zealand begins and ends with the sea. Understand that and you understand New Zealanders."
— Maurice Shadbolt

Tucked away in the South Pacific, Aotearoa New Zealand is an island nation with four million people of Maori, Pacific Island, European and, increasingly, Asian extraction. A mountainous land of glaciated peaks, active volcanoes and rolling country, New Zealand is constantly being dramatically changed by the forces of nature. Bound by the Tasman Sea to the West and the vast Pacific Ocean to the East, this dynamic landscape is steeply tilted towards its coastal fringe. All-up, there are 11,000 km of breathtakingly beautiful beaches, clifftops and forest-fringed seascapes to grace this 'land of the long white cloud'.

New Zealand stretches southward from 34 degrees South latitude at Cape Reinga near the tip of the North Island to 47 degrees South at the southernmost point of Stewart Island. The coasts are influenced by a maritime climate ranging from subtropical in Northland to cool-temperate in Southland. Across Foveaux Strait, sparsely populated Stewart Island is a synthesis of climate, environment, flora and fauna, combining the best of South Island forest landscape with the delicate ecosystems of the sub-Antarctic

◀ *Sunset lights up clouds over the Seaward Kaikoura Mountains and the limestone rocks on the foreshore. Kaikoura was once a whaling station but is now the dolphin and whale watching capital of New Zealand.*

islands. Much of Stewart Island is set aside as Rakiura National Park and its shores are among the least impacted wilderness areas anywhere in the country.

Beyond these shores, New Zealand's farthest-flung territories span the sub-tropical to the sub-Antarctic. One thousand kilometres to the northeast of the North Island, the remote, uninhabited, volcanic Kermadec Island group is both a protected nature reserve (landing by permit only) and, offshore, New Zealand's largest marine reserve. In contrast to the lush sub-tropical vegetation of the Kermadecs, the blustery Chatham Islands lie 800 km eastward of the South Island. These storm-swept islands have farming and fishing communities that endure an unforgiving climate. The outlying Chathams' islands are an important breeding ground for albatrosses and other seabirds.

At times, New Zealand's sub-Antarctic islands are even more tempestuous than the Chathams, though these rigorously managed reserves are justly famous for their wildlife-rich coastlines. On the fringe of the Southern Ocean, barely a few hundred kilometres south of Stewart Island, these uninhabited groups of wind-lashed islands include the Snares (Tini Heke), Auckland (Motu Maha) and Campbell (Motu Ihupuku), all specially-protected sub-Antarctic environments that are designated World Heritage Sites by UNESCO.

New Zealand's most remote coastlines outside Antarctica's Ross Dependency are the penguin and albatross-crowded outcrops of the Bounty and Antipodes Islands, mere specks in the Southern Ocean and a long way off the southeast coast of the South Island. Seen as a whole, all these island groups are ecologically and economically important to New Zealand, a country whose marine environment is 15 times larger than its terrestrial area. As a result, New Zealand's Exclusive Economic Zone is the fourth largest in the world.

New Zealand has a relatively young but volatile geological history beginning with the break-up of the supercontinent Gondwanaland. Some 70 million years ago the landmass of what is now New Zealand became isolated from the continents including Antarctica. Then, as sea levels rose at the end of the last ice age about 10,000 years ago, the three main islands gradually took their present-day shape. New Zealand is located on the boundary between two continental plates, the Indo-Australian and the Pacific. The relentless collision of these plates created New Zealand's Alpine Fault that continues to jolt and grind away beneath a giant diagonal slash across the country. Plate movement also generates the North Island's active volcanoes as well as perpetuates the uprising of the Southern Alps. Unsurprisingly, this unbridled power has an enormous influence on the shaping of New Zealand's coasts.

For Maori, a Polynesian people of skilled navigators who arrived in New Zealand sometime between 1150 and 1350, the country simply owes its existence to Maui, a demi-god who lived in the ancestral homeland of Hawaiiki. One day, while out with his brothers in a waka, Maui's fishhook snared Te Ika a Maui, the fish of Maui. As the catch was brought to the surface and beaten with clubs, it formed the convoluted shape of the North Island. The South Island became known as Te Waka a Maui (Maui's waka) while Stewart Island, the waka's anchor, is Te Punga a Maui.

According to tribal narratives, Kupe, a great fisherman, was the first Polynesian to reach New Zealand shores. Eventually the Maori settled widely in coastal regions, principally in the North Island though also in the South Island's Kaikoura, Banks Peninsula, Otago and West Coast regions. During the 1500s, the Moriori people voyaged from New Zealand to the Chathams, developing a distinct culture there.

The Maori and early European navigators who chanced upon New Zealand's coastline interacted violently at times. The Dutch

▶ *A launch leaves the sheltered bay near Castlepoint lighthouse at sunrise, Wairarapa coast.*

explorer Abel Tasman is credited with 'discovering' New Zealand in 1642, however four of his crewmen were killed during an encounter with Maori at Murderer's Bay in the South Island's Golden Bay.

Then, in 1769, Englishman Captain James Cook in *Endeavour* landed at Poverty Bay in the Bay of Plenty and this time several Maori were killed in skirmishes. Cook subsequently charted much of New Zealand's coastline, though he surmised that Banks Peninsula was probably an island (named after his naturalist Joseph Banks). After rounding the southern tip of Stewart Island he also wrongly assumed that the island was an extension of the South Island. Cook landed at many sites including Ship's Cove in Queen Charlotte Sounds. In January 1770, from nearby Arapawa Island at the tip of the South Island, Cook looked into the strait between the South and North Islands that now bears his name.

In 1772 and 1777, with the ships *Resolution* and *Adventure*, Cook made two more voyages to New Zealand as part of his quest to locate the great southern continent (terra australis incognita). In the autumn of 1773, after an arduous voyage towards Antarctica, Cook landed in Fiordland's Dusky Sound so he could make observations to fix the geographical position of New Zealand. The stumps of trees felled at Astronomer Point in Pickersgill Harbour can still be seen.

By the late 18th century, with Maori well established around the coast, there came a steady stream of European sailors, missionaries and traders who built and occupied settlements. In 1840 the Treaty of Waitangi was signed between the British Crown and various Maori chiefs, bringing New Zealand into the British Empire and giving Maori equal rights with British citizens. Even now, aspects of this watershed agreement are still being ironed out.

Modern-day New Zealanders, be they Maori or Pakeha (originally Europeans but now, simply, non-Maori), all love the sea. As few live far from the coast, beach culture is deeply embedded in every New Zealander's psyche. Everyone feels that unrestricted access to the foreshores has been enshrined as part of their heritage.

A great many New Zealanders spend every spare moment relaxing at the family's modest holiday home – the bach (pronounced batch, a 'batchelor pad'), or, to Southlanders, a crib. Many baches have purposely been equipped with only basic facilities, so that life can be pared down and enjoyed for its simple pleasures. Christmas, ironically at the peak of summer, is traditionally spent at the bach or at least celebrated with friends at a beach picnic. As the society has become wealthier or is influenced by foreign investment, the humble Kiwi bach is slowly disappearing, often being replaced by luxurious homes that stand empty for much of the year.

Whatever their age or ethnic background, New Zealanders continue to be drawn to the coast both for its therapeutic powers and, for some, the potential that a day's fishing could result in a feed for the family. Others are passionate about their favourite surfing beach. Scuba divers and snorkellers too, cherish their regular dive spots, perhaps in a sheltered bay or at one of New Zealand's 30 'no-take' marine reserves. Surfcast fishing from the beach or from a rock platform is an extremely popular pastime throughout the community.

New Zealand has long been renowned as an agricultural nation, with sheep, beef, wine and kiwifruit being vital to its export economy. A growing number of New Zealanders also earn a living from the sea, with some harvesting oyster, mussel or lobster beds close to the coast while others catch pelagic fin fish in deeper waters.

New Zealanders are ardent participants in sports and recreational activities ranging from rugby and cricket to yachting and mountaineering. There is also a growing number of hard-bitten

▶ *East Cape lighthouse is the most easterly point of New Zealand. This visitor to the North Island's wild and relatively uninhabited coastal region of Eastland is enjoying a view out into the Pacific Ocean.*

endurance athletes who delight in racing towards the coast in events such as the Mountains to the Sea. One running-biking-kayaking marathon in the South Island traverses from the West coast to the East, all in under 12 gruelling hours.

But it is to the delightfully warm Northland and the Bay of Islands where the less driven are attracted. Only a few hours' drive north of Auckland, this tranquil part of New Zealand is about as close to paradise as it comes. It is also surprisingly wild and natural without the highrise development commonly associated with holiday destinations overseas. The many small rural settlements fringed by clean yellow sand beaches are a delight for a weekend sojourn by city-bound New Zealanders and overseas visitors alike. Justly famous, the sand dunes at Ninety Mile Beach on Northland's west coast are remarkable for their sheer scale and rippled natural texture. Another frequently visited spot on this coastline is the Cape Reinga lighthouse. Reinga is at the confluence of the Tasman Sea and Pacific Ocean and, significantly, it is sacred to Maori for it is from here that the spirits of the dead are set free to depart on their journey to the ancestral Hawaiiki.

The Bay of Islands, on the east coast of Northland, features a myriad of tiny islands notable for their safe anchorages – definitely a 'must visit' for both yachties and holidaymakers. Big-game fishermen have also been drawn here ever since the 1920s when an awareness of the region's attributes became recognised internationally. Few have written so eloquently of the attractions of fishing for black marlin and swordfish than the flamboyant American Zane Grey in his 1926 book *Tales of the Angler's Eldorado*.

The Bay of Islands is also famous for the picturesque township of Russell (Kororareka), the first capital of New Zealand and one of the first European settlements. During the 1800s Russell (described as the 'hellhole of the South Pacific') was a major port to resupply European and American vessels involved in whaling and the export of kauri timber. Twenty-two kilometres offshore, northeast of Whangarei, lie Northland's Poor Knights Islands, a marine reserve and world-class dive spot.

The shores of the Hauraki Gulf and Coromandel Peninsula close to the 'city of sails', Auckland, are probably the 'hottest', most expensive real estate sites in New Zealand. But this urban development also sits on no less than 50 volcanoes, the most famous of which, Rangitoto Island, last erupted 600 years ago. Today, Rangitoto is a scenic reserve and home to a large pohutukawa forest, New Zealand's iconic red flowering Christmas tree. In sharp contrast to the semi-tropical eastern seaboard, the west coast close to Auckland has, in general, potentially treacherous beaches, with strong currents and powerful surf. After crossing the Waitakere Ranges, Piha Beach offers classically shaped waves, a major attraction for the experienced surfing fraternity.

Every summer, Coromandel Peninsula draws visitors by the thousands. It is hard to resist the intimate beaches complete with caves and archways to dash through at low tide, terrific body surfing and cool forest walks along cliff edges draped in pohutukawa blossoms. Again this part of New Zealand is a product of volcanic eruption. The cataclysmic Taupo eruption 2000 years ago that burst from the centre of the North Island helped shape both the Coromandel and the entire Bay of Plenty to the south. Apart from visits to Rotorua and the volcanic plateau, one of the best ways to experience active volcanism is to take a helicopter or launch to the marine volcano White Island, 50km offshore from the Bay of Plenty township of Whakatane.

Dawn comes first to New Zealand on the summit of Mt Hikurangi, 1754 metres, highest point in the Raukumara Range and said to be the resting place for Maui's waka. Hikurangi and the region around East Cape lighthouse is collectively called Eastland, very much Maori heartland. This wind-battered coast is where the first Maori voyagers put ashore and, later, in 1769, at Poverty bay near Gisborne, where Maori's bloody encounter took place with Captain Cook. Bathed in soft light and framed by muted green forests and scrub-choked headlands, Eastland is coast that remains spiritually wild and free.

Eastland's Hawke's Bay city of Napier is known as the art deco capital of New Zealand, though its volcanic black sand beaches and hinterland of vineyards and kiwifruit orchards also add a charm to the region. Visitors too, flock to the nearby Australian gannet colony of 5000 breeding pairs at Cape Kidnappers (Te Matau-a-Maui, Maui's fishhook but called Kidnappers by Cook after Maori tried to abduct a crewman). For those who like isolated coastlines to explore then the stretch southward along the Wairarapa coast to Cape Palliser is hard to beat. On the way, a pre-dawn climb to the headland above Castlepoint lighthouse (built 1913) is a must for early risers.

Roaming southward down the North Island's west coast, Raglan Beach, due West of Hamilton, is a heart-stopper for surfies. Then, all the way around the Taranaki coast to Wanganui there are breathtaking vistas of surf dumping onto black-sand beaches topped by ochre, green and yellow-striped cliffs and archways. These dramatic seascapes are framed by an equally dramatic backdrop of ice-encrusted volcano, Mt Taranaki – New Zealand coastline at its best.

And if North Island coasts are a delight, then those in the South Island are simply dazzling. With the benefit of a lower population, the South Island and its beaches have been able to retain a real sense of tranquillity and naturalness. Strict land management ensures that private baches, national park huts and tourism lodges located on the coast have been sited tastefully so that they blend almost seamlessly into the environment. The visual impact of signage, buildings and tracks has been minimised by careful landscaping or softening with tree ferns and nikau palms.

▶ *North Taranaki's coastal cliffs at Tongaporutu are often battered by storms and huge waves that come in from the Tasman Sea.*

▲ *Otanarito Beach on Banks Peninsula is close to the famous seaside holiday resort of Akaroa and its shallow waters make it a popular place for families to take small children. This is the last bay on the Banks Peninsula walkway before climbing up through Hinewai Nature Reserve to the road above Akaroa.*

◄ *Sunset is a special time at Mason Bay in Stewart Island's Rakiura National Park. The remoteness of Rakiura's west coast beaches means that visitors can enjoy the solitude of long beach walks with the possibility of seeing kiwi in the extensive sand dune zone.*

There is, however, a marked contrast between the rawness and open expanses of West Coast beaches and the more sheltered nature of those in the North, around Marlborough Sounds, Abel Tasman National Park and Golden Bay. And, down the east coast there is a definite otherworldly charm and intimacy to the bays on Canterbury's Banks Peninsula and on the Otago Peninsula near Dunedin. The Catlins coastline in Southland is the gateway to another climatic zone that, at times, seems only a step away from the sub-Antarctic. Yet, on a windless day, the hidden gems of bays around the Southland coast can almost appear Polynesian.

As I have long been enamoured of snow-covered mountains, my favourite South Island coastal haunt is unquestionably Kaikoura, an easy two-hour drive North of Christchurch. The Seaward Kaikoura range rears abruptly behind the busy township of Kaikoura, with its winter mantle of snow glowing rose pink in the morning sun. Once a whaling station, and still a fishing port, Kaikoura has also transformed itself into the whale and dolphin-watching centre of New Zealand, and the fur seals pups are pretty cute too.

Sperm whales and other cetaceans such as humpbacks and even blue whales flip their tails skywards before sounding to feed in the food-rich waters of the 2000-metre deep Hikurangi Trench. Close encounters with whales and various dolphin species including large pods of orca, dusky and Hectors occur routinely, observed from the dedicated craft with their knowledgeable guides.

One of the most memorable treats of a South Island sojourn is to don a wetsuit and actually swim with the dolphins at Kaikoura. This unique experience is also on offer at Akaroa, a one-time French establishment on Banks Peninsula, but now a charming tourist village close to Christchurch. The Banks Peninsula Walkway (starts and finishes in Akaroa) and its cousin, the Kaikoura Coastal Walkway, are both splendid ways to combine a three-day tramp with the hospitality of farmer's lodges and spectacular panoramas.

After a visit to watch the dawn rise behind the spherical Moeraki boulders south of Oamaru, the Otago Peninsula is definitely worth exploring. Apart from Otago's gorgeous scenery and hidden nooks of beaches, it is a privilege to see both the majestic Royal albatross in flight and the furtive Yellow-eyed penguins scurry over sand dunes. Then it is time to lose yourself in a forest walk in the Catlins or launch out onto one of its lonely headlands above pounding surf.

I also love the West Coast beaches. The distinctive nikau palms, tree ferns and nodding toe toe grasses greatly enhance the network of coastal walks available from north of the Punakaiki blowholes in Paparoa National Park to beyond Karamea and the Heaphy Track (Kahurangi National Park). To top it off, the route from south of Hokitika through to Haast Pass past the Franz Josef and Fox Glacier villages offers some of the best scenery in New Zealand. It is simply awe-inspiring to stand on the driftwood on Gillespie's beach near Fox and watch the sun set on New Zealand's highest summits, Aoraki/Mt Cook and Tasman.

As part of UNESCO's World Heritage Te Wahipounamu region, Fiordland is one of the largest and most precious national parks and wilderness regions on Earth. Its rugged coastlines and deeply incised fjords look as if they've been cut out by a gigantic fretsaw. Equally precious and just across Foveaux Strait lies Rakiura National Park, focal point of Stewart Island.

Touching down on the long sandy beach at Mason Bay after a short flight in a small plane from Invercargill, I sensed I had entered a world apart. I had flown past Codfish Island, a sanctuary devoted to bringing the ungainly kakapo parrot back from the brink of extinction. Then, as I scrambled up the dunes to watch the sun disappear into the Tasman Sea, I followed a set of Kiwi tracks. Stalking the Kiwi spoor were the unmistakable paw prints of a feral cat. I offered a silent prayer that New Zealand will soon eradicate its wild cats, stoats and ferrets so that Kiwi, Yellow-eyed penguins and other endangered birds may flourish once more. I prayed too, that everyone will cherish New Zealand's coastal landscape and marine ecosystems and treat them with the respect they deserve.

Colin Monteath

▶ *Cape Maria van Diemen lies just south of Cape Reinga, the northernmost point of New Zealand where the Tasman and Pacific Oceans meet. Northland is blessed with extensive, clean sand beaches that are fringed by native vegetation.*

▲ How special for these children to ride their horses down to a Northland beach so they can go surfing.

◀ Sand ripples on dunes typify the cleanliness of New Zealand's beaches. Plastic debris washed overboard from fishing vessels however, cannot be ignored as a growing form of pollution around New Zealand's coasts.

▶ Children delight in sand surfing on the massive dunes at Te Paki that lie behind Northland's Ninety Mile Beach.

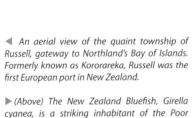

◀ An aerial view of the quaint township of Russell, gateway to Northland's Bay of Islands. Formerly known as Kororareka, Russell was the first European port in New Zealand.

▶ (Above) The New Zealand Bluefish, Girella cyanea, is a striking inhabitant of the Poor Knights Islands Marine Reserve that can weigh up to 9kg. (Below) The blue-eyed triplefin, Notoclinops segmentalus, is another of the beautiful New Zealand coastal fish species found at Anne's Reef, Poor Knights Islands Marine Reserve.

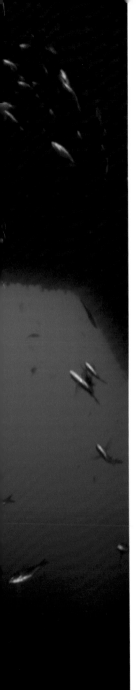

▲ *Divers prepare to descend into the clear waters off Great Barrier Island near Auckland. Great Barrier is justly famous for its diving, snorkelling, walking, surfing and kayaking..*

◄ *A school of demoiselle fish (Chromis dispulis) swirl around a diver at the Poor Knights Islands Marine Reserve, 24km off the east coast of Northland. Poor Knights was gazetted in 1981, New Zealand's second marine reserve.*

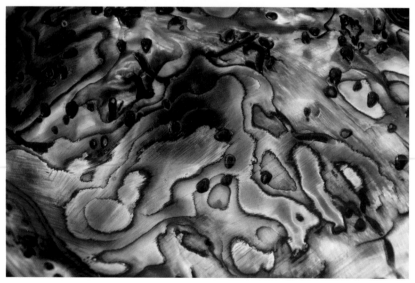

◄ (Above) Sunset shells, *Gari stangerei*, also known as kuwharu are commonly found on North Island beaches such as Whitianga on the Coromandel Peninsula. (Below) The polished surface of the common paua shell, *Haliotis iris*, radiates colours that somehow have a distinct New Zealand glow to them.

▶ Silhouetted by the evening light, a surfer crosses the shallows of Muriwai's black sand beach west of Auckland. Always in search of the perfect wave, surfers from all over the world are now attracted to New Zealand beaches for their small though finely-shaped waves and fun-loving surf culture.

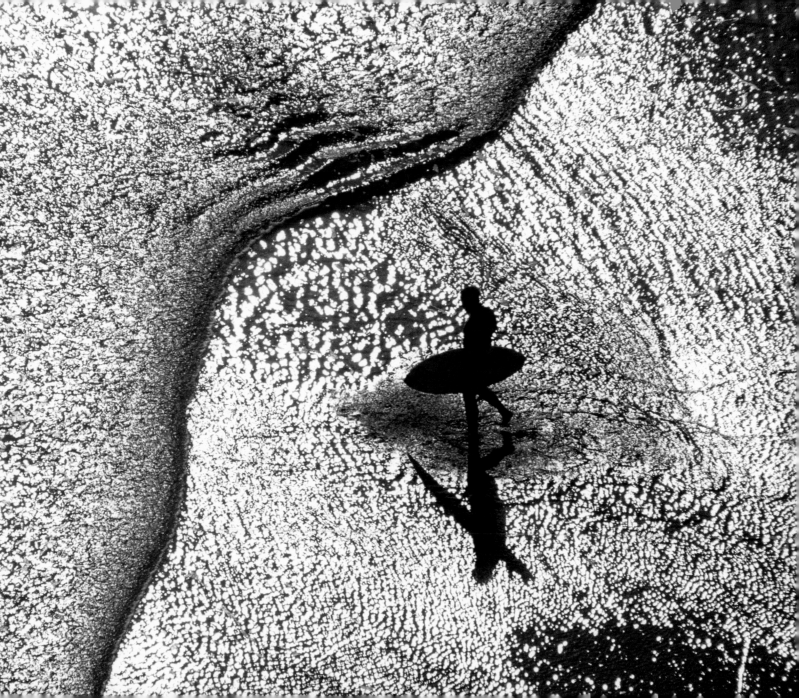

◀ Rays from the setting sun filter through the clouds to cast a pinkish glow on the gannet colony at Muriwai, west of Auckland.

▶ Dawn light glows around the 600-year-old volcano on Rangitoto Island near Auckland. Rangitoto is the largest and youngest of the 50 volcanoes around Auckland and the island is now managed by New Zealand's Department of Conservation as a reserve.

▲ Hot Water Beach at Hahei on the Coromandel Peninsula attracts many visitors every day. Even if it is overcast or raining it is relaxing to dig a pit in the sand and immerse yourself in the geothermally heated water.

◀ Cathedral Cove on the Coromandel Peninsula is an extremely popular beach for relaxing on as well as for body surfing. In early December, the steep cliffs overhanging the beach are draped with clusters of flowers on the pohutukawa trees.

▲ Pohutukawa trees in flower during early December are one of the most beautiful aspects of the Coromandel Peninsula as the trees grow right on the edge of the white sand beaches. (Right) Snorkellers prepare to enter the water to explore Gemstone Bay, near Cathedral Cove on the Coromandel Peninsula.

◄ Intimate beaches of the Coromandel Peninsula, such as these ones at Cathedral Cove, are fun to explore, with tunnels formed in the overhanging cliffs a delight to race through between waves.

◀ A rockclimber tackles a steep crack line on Pohutukawa Cliff, Te Ananui Bay, Coromandel Peninsula.

▶ Coromandel Peninsula is noted for its fine sunrises and sunsets that enrich seascapes discovered during a lone walk along a beach.

▲ Pohutukawa, Metrosideros excelsa, is commonly called the New Zealand Christmas tree. The crimson florets add a touch of vivid colour to many New Zealand beachfronts, especially in the North Island.

◀ It is well worth going up Mount Paku on the Coromandel Peninsula for this fine view out across Tairua Harbour, especially when the pohutukawa tree is in flower during December.

◀ The lookout on Mount Maunganui provides good views down onto the caravan park and township beside Ocean Beach.

▶ An aerial view taken over Papamoa of Mount Maunganui and Ocean Beach. To the north lies the Bay of Plenty's Matakana Island.

▲ Near East Cape it is not hard to find a place to park your caravan. If you don't need neighbours for a few nights then Eastland is a great place to visit.

◀ Although it lies in the heartland of the North Island, East Cape and Eastland is a rugged and isolated coast that retains a unique New Zealand feeling of wildness. This dirt road winds its way along beside Kaiaua Beach not far from the regional centre of Gisborne.

▶ Built in 1894 in Papatea Bay near East Cape, Raukokore's Anglican Christ Church is lit up at dusk as the setting sun shines through its windows.

◀ A young woman rides her horse along the edge of the surf on a beach near Gisborne.

▶ A horse roaming free above an Eastland beach near East Cape lighthouse. Horses are still used for hunting in the backcountry by many who live along on this rugged coastline.

◀ An expert board surfer flips his board around on the crest of this wave at Wainui Beach near Gisborne.

▶ (Above) A young female surfer turns into a perfect wave at Wainui Beach in Eastland. (Below) Surf lifesavers power their inflatable craft through a wave during rescue practice at Wainui Beach near Gisborne. Most lifesavers in New Zealand belong to volunteer organizations and train hard every weekend, thereby helping tremendously to keep the beaches safe.

◀ *The muted pinks of dawn add a soft glow to this wave-smoothed mudstone boulder that lies on the black sand Waihua Beach in northern Hawke's Bay.*

▶ *Courting gannets preen each other with their bills at Cape Kidnappers gannet colony, Hawke's Bay.*

◀ *Sunset through the Three Sisters, a famous landmark on the Tongaporutu coastline, North Taranaki.*

▶ *Taranaki's wild and windy Tongaporutu's coast can best be viewed from the Whitecliff's Walkway.*

◀ *Viewed from the Whitecliff's Walkway, wave-sculpted sandstone cliffs feature deep caverns along the Tongaporutu black sand beach coastline.*

▶ *Viewed from Tongaporutu, twilight adds a soft glow to Taranaki's volcano Mt Egmont/Taranaki and, to the right, the Pouakai Range.*

▲ *A rainbow over the Castlepoint lighthouse on the beautiful Wairarapa coast.*

◄ *A boardwalk winds down to the Castlepoint lighthouse and beach on the Wairarapa coastline.*

◄ *(Above) Opal top shells, also known as Matamatangongo, Microlenchus species. (Below) Scallop shells.*

▶ *Viewed across The Cook Strait at sunset, the South Island ranges appear in silhouette in this panorama from Island Bay, Wellington.*

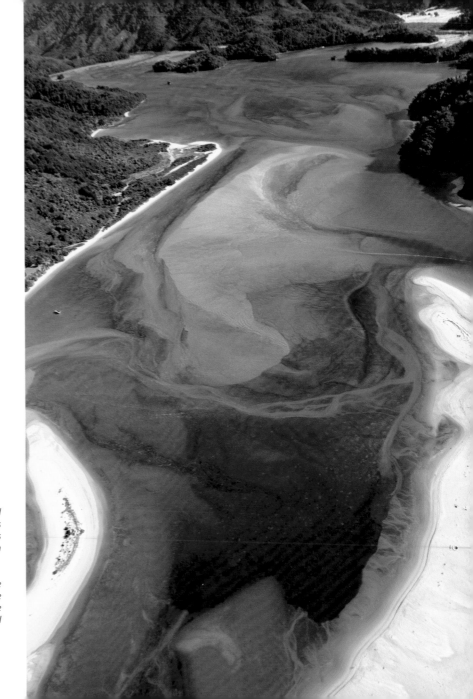

◀ New Zealand's distinctively shaped cabbage tree, *Cordyline australis*, is silhouetted against evening colours in this seascape from Alligator Head of the South Island's tranquil Marlborough Sounds.

▶ This aerial view of Awaroa Inlet in the Nelson district gives an indication of the clarity and cleanliness of the both the water and sand in Abel Tasman National Park.

◀ Sea kayaking around the many bays and inlets of Abel Tasman National Park is as popular now as walking along the trails through the forest that link the glorious white sand beaches.

▶ New Zealand fur seal pups delight in playing with the sea kayakers who silently approach the seal breeding colonies in Abel Tasman National Park.

◀ 'Take nothing but photographs, leave nothing but footprints'... the old cliché remains true throughout New Zealand but especially here on a pristine golden sand beach at Kohaihai River mouth on the Heaphy Track, Kahurangi National Park.

▶ The 78km Heaphy Track in Kahurangi National Park is perhaps New Zealand's finest coastal walk. Here, two women encounter juvenile cormorants on Scott's Beach at the Karamea end of the track. Soon, they will leave the nikau palm fringed beaches and climb up into higher forest country as they head towards the Nelson end of the walk.

◀ *Evening light casts delicate reflections of the Archway islands on Wharariki Beach, a popular Golden Bay attraction.*

▶ *This aerial view of Wainui Inlet gives an indication of the beauty to be found throughout the Golden Bay district at the northern tip of the South Island.*

▲ Organic matter creates an unusual detail of nature after being washed up on a beach near Karamea on the South Island's West Coast.

◀ As the sun sinks into the Tasman Sea, nikau palms are silhouetted near the start of the Heaphy Track, Kahurangi National Park. The nikau palm, Rhopalostylis sapida, is the southernmost member of the palm family and the only palm endemic to New Zealand.

▲ *Sunset light sparkles off the surf and cliff edges along Te Miko Bay, Paparoa National Park.*

◄ *Evening light illuminates the nikau palms and boulders on this Heaphy Track beach, Kahurangi National Park.*

▲ *Blowholes like this one near Truman's Track are a major feature of the Punakaiki coastline in Paparoa National Park.*

▶ *Nikau palms seen here just north of Punakaiki township give the Paparoa National Park the feeling of being almost tropical.*

▲ *Kelp washed up under the cliffs below Truman's Track. At low tide, Truman track and beach are a popular short walk close to the township of Punakaiki, Paparoa National Park.*

▶ *The blowhole at Punakaiki's Pancake Rocks is really spectacular when a storm lashes the West Coast of the South Island.*

▲▲ *A wandering albatross, Diomedea exulans, in flight close to the Kaikoura coast.*

◀ *The Kaikoura Peninsula in North Canterbury, with the snow-covered Seaward Kaikoura Mountains behind, sticks out into the Pacific Ocean at a place where there is a deep trench in the seafloor. The upwelling of currents close to the coast means that there is abundant food for the whales, dolphins, seals and seabirds that populate this part of the South Island coastline.*

▶ *A sperm whale, Physeter macrocephalus, sounds at sunset near the township of Kaikoura. Once hunted from a shore-based whaling operation at Kaikoura, sperm whales and other cetaceans now enjoy total protection in New Zealand waters.*

▲ New Zealand fur seals, Arctocephalus forsterii, are in abundance along the Kaikoura coastline. In recent years, these beautiful marine mammals have become a major attraction to visitors initially drawn to Kaikoura for a whale or dolphin encounter.

◄ Dawn over the Seaward Kaikoura Mountains adds a pink glow to the foreshore of creamy-coloured limestone rocks, a feature of Kaikoura Bay.

◀ *Two women view the long cliffline and beach that lead up to the Seaward Kaikoura Mountains. This vantage point is part of the increasingly popular Kaikoura Walkway that traverses delightful hill, farm and coastal environments.*

▶ *Dusky dolphins, Lagenorhynchus obscurus, cavort underwater just off the Kaikoura coast. Kaikoura is now the whale and dolphin centre of New Zealand. Swimming with dolphins has become one of the truly great natural experiences to be had in New Zealand.*

◀ *A woman reels in a fish through the surf just south of Kaikoura. Part of the snow-covered Seaward Kaikoura Mountains lies behind. Surfcasting is a major activity for many New Zealand families while on holiday.*

▶ *A pod of Dusky dolphins plays off Kaikoura Heads just after dawn.*

The Kaikoura Walkway provides superb coastal views just south of Kaikoura on day two of this easy though dramatic three-day excursion. In the space of a few kilometres a walker experiences rolling hill country with a backdrop of snowy peaks, rich farmlands and empty near-pristine beaches.

▲ The canopies of these old matai trees are being blown about as a strong southerly wind hits Canterbury's Banks Peninsula above Gough's Bay near Akaroa.

▶ A walker on the Bank's Peninsula Walkway looks on as sheep are mustered into yards for shearing at Flea Bay. Commonly, around the Banks Peninsula coast, pods of Hector's dolphins can be spotted. The Hector's is endemic to New Zealand waters and is the smallest of the dolphin family.

▲ *Juvenile spotted shags crowd along the old wharf behind Oamaru historic quarter as dawn lights up storm clouds over the Pacific Ocean.*

◄ *The spotted shag colony at Kakanui in North Otago being blasted by strong winds and the coastal cliffs pounded by big waves.*

▲ Moeraki boulders at dawn, south of Oamaru, North Otago. Maori legend links the origin of these unusual spherical boulders with the arrival of their migration canoes. A canoe ran aground here and the boulders are said to be their food provisions turned to stone.

◀ Children ride their horses along the Moeraki boulder beach. Moeraki is a small coastal fishing village that also caters for bach owners and holiday-makers wanting a quiet weekend.

▶ Nugget Point lighthouse is a popular destination from which to to witness the dawn during a visit to Otago's windswept Catlins Coast. The Catlins stretch from Dunedin southward along the coast towards Southland at the southern tip of the South Island. The rare and elusive yellow-eyed penguin, New Zealand (Hooker's) sea lions, and even the occasional leopard seal can be seen along this magnificent coast.

◀ A lone figure strolls quietly along a West Coast beach near Haast, not far from the main highway that links Wanaka with Fox and Franz Josef Glaciers. Thick bush commonly comes right to the beach edge, adding to the feeling of remoteness and solitude, treasured attributes of a South Island sojourn.

▶ Rimu trees, Decrydium cupressinum, are reflected in a small pond above the beach at Bruce Bay, in South Westland.

◀ Evening light casts a warm glow across the beach beneath Knight's Point, South Westland.

▶ Makawhio (Jacob's) River mouth enters the Tasman Sea with the sweep of South Westland's Bruce Bay beyond.

▲ *A mother and daughter paddle their sea kayak on Doubtful Sound, one of Fiordland National Park's most special fjords. Though rain and sandflies are forces to be reckoned with in Fiordland, the region features numerous unique coastal landscapes, with thick forest coming steeply down to the water's edge.*

▶ *Mitre Peak reflected in Fiordland's Milford Sound is perhaps the most recognisable panorama in New Zealand.*

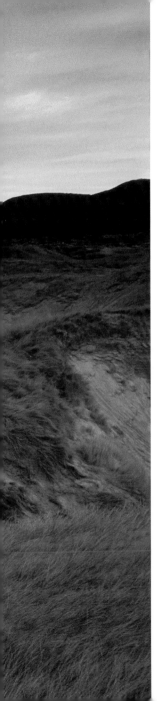

▲Stewart Island kiwi or tokoeka, Apteryx australis lawry, can be viewed at night on Ocean Beach as they fossick about in the seaweed for sandhoppers.

◄ Mason Bay in Rakiura National Park is one of Stewart Island's most beautiful coastal regions with extensive areas of giant sand dunes backed by thick manuka scrub. For those keen on tramping, deer hunting and fishing Mason Bay is paradise. Kiwi also inhabit the strip of dunes behind the beach.

◀ A tramper enjoys a late afternoon panorama looking down on The Gutter at the southern end of Mason Bay, Rakiura National Park.

▶ The hoiho or Yellow-eyed penguin, Megadyptes antipodes, remains the most endangered of all the 17 penguin species, in part due to predation by dogs and cats. Naturally, they are totally protected around the New Zealand coastline however their main stronghold is in the Auckland Island sub-Antarctic Island group south of Stewart Island.

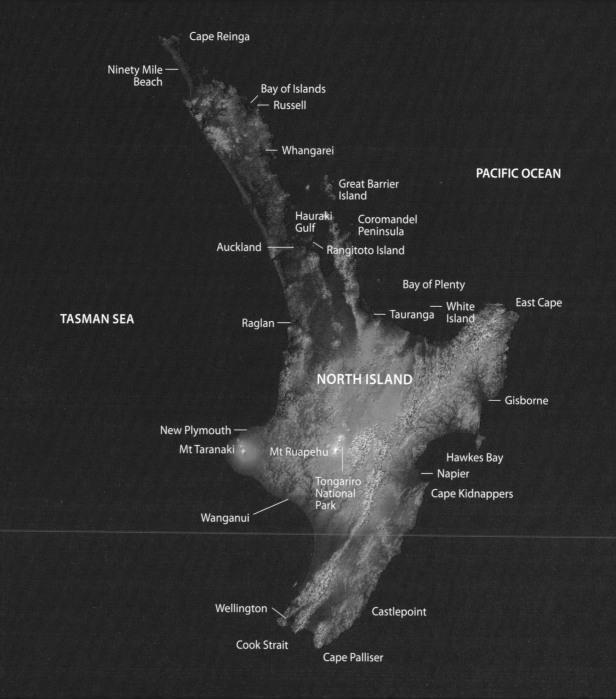

Cape Reinga

Ninety Mile
Beach

Bay of Islands
Russell

Whangarei

PACIFIC OCEAN

Great Barrier
Island

Hauraki
Gulf

Coromandel
Peninsula

Auckland

Rangitoto Island

Bay of Plenty

East Cape

TASMAN SEA

Raglan

Tauranga

White
Island

NORTH ISLAND

Gisborne

New Plymouth

Mt Taranaki

Mt Ruapehu

Hawkes Bay
Napier

Tongariro
National
Park

Cape Kidnappers

Wanganui

Wellington

Castlepoint

Cook Strait

Cape Palliser

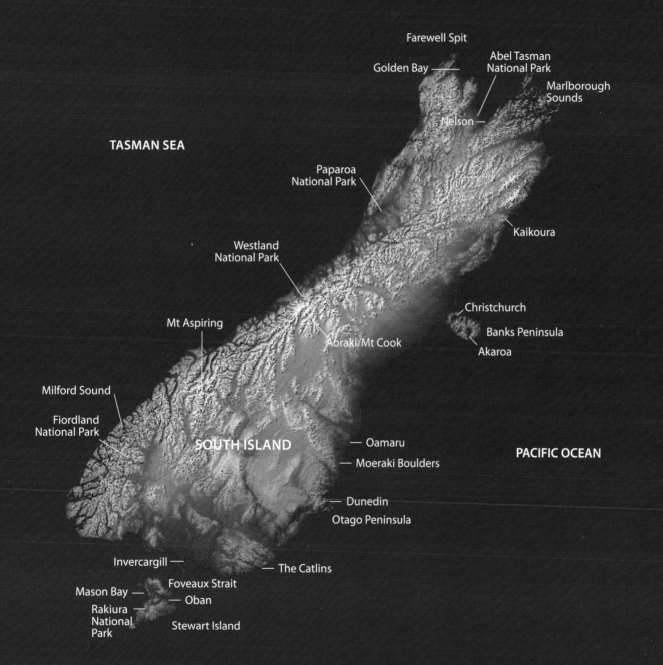

Farewell Spit

Golden Bay

Abel Tasman
National Park

Marlborough
Sounds

Nelson

TASMAN SEA

Paparoa
National Park

Kaikoura

Westland
National Park

Christchurch

Mt Aspiring

Banks Peninsula

Aoraki/Mt Cook

Akaroa

Milford Sound

Fiordland
National Park

SOUTH ISLAND

Oamaru

PACIFIC OCEAN

Moeraki Boulders

Dunedin

Otago Peninsula

Invercargill

The Catlins

Foveaux Strait

Mason Bay

Oban

Rakiura
National
Park

Stewart Island

Colin Monteath: Page 5, 9, 12, 13, 15, 17, 26, 27, 28, 29b, 34, 37b, 39, 41a, 57, 65, 66, 70, 71, 72, 74, 76, 77, 78, 79, 81, 83, 84, 88, 89, 90, 92, Back cover. John Rendle: Cover, 16a, 37a, 49, 60, 82a. Andy Reisinger: 2, 4, 17, 25, 31, 33, 51. Harley Betts: 1, 11, 42, 44, 46, 47, 48, 52, 86, 87. Peter & Lynda Harper: Endpapers, 7, 8, 22a & b, 43, 50a & b, 61, 96. Ross & Diane Armstrong: 19a & b, 20. Andy Belcher: 21. Logan Murray: 16b, 38, 40. Peter Morath: 18, 32, 35, 45, 59, 80, 82b. David Hallett: 23. Jim Harding: 24, 56, 63. Graham Charles: 29a, 55. Mark Jones: 30. Rob Brown: 36, 58, 62, 64, 67, 68, 85, 91. Ross Nolly: 48. Guy Vickers: 49. Grant Stirling: 53, 54. Jason Elsworth: 69a. Steve Dawson: 69b, 73. Barbara Todd: 75. Tui De Roy: 93.

▲ *The cross-section of a nautilus shell reveals a glorious mix of colours from delicate shades of orange to mauve.*